POLLY TOYNBEE

Polly Toynbee is one of the country's most respected journalists whose career has not just displayed a unique clarity of vision but an acute understanding of life in the late 20th century.

Polly was educated at Badminton School, Holland Park Comprehensive and St Anne's College, Oxford, where she read history.

She joined *The Observer* in 1968 as a reporter and feature writer and over the next eight years began to build her reputation as one of the nation's leading journalists. She moved to *The Guardian* in 1977 and as a key member of the newspaper's editorial team was voted Columnist of the Year on three separate occasions in the prestigious British Press Awards.

While her writing had already become familiar to readers across the world, it was not until 1988 as Social Affairs Editor for BBC News and Current Affairs did Polly become a familiar face to millions of viewers. In 1995 she became Associate Editor of *The Independent.*

Her work is not confined to the columns and broadcast channels of the media, she has written a novel and reference books on unskilled labour, the National Health Service and adoption.

Widowed with four children, Polly Toynbee lives in London.

The Future of Care for
Older People

before the last date

Sarah Gibbs Memorial Lecture Series

The Future of Care
for Older People
Facing up to Society's Choices

POLLY TOYNBEE

Lemos & Crane
in association with The Friendship Group

Published in Great Britain 1996 by
Lemos & Crane
20 Pond Square, Highgate
London N6 6BA

in association with

The Friendship Group
17-19 Braithwaite Road
Birmingham B11 1LB

© The Friendship Group 1996

ISBN 1-898001-21-9

A CIP catalogue record for this book is available
from the British Library

Designed by Mick Keates

Front cover photograph by John Cass

Photograph of Polly Toynbee
The Independent/Edward Sykes

Typeset by Concise Artisans, London

Printed by Redwood Books, Trowbridge

CONTENTS

FOREWORD

Professor Nicholas Deakin

This publication is important not just for its own considerable merits. It is significant because both in its subject matter and in the approach that she chose to adopt, Polly Toynbee underlines the way in which fundamental changes are now taking place in our society.

More particularly, the topic of community care illustrates how the voluntary sector has taken on a whole range of additional responsibilities for the delivery of services. Fifty years ago, it seemed as if the steady advance of the state in all areas of social services would make much voluntary sector provision redundant. In fact, the take-over by the statutory sector was never as comprehensive as subsequent legend suggests. However, there was never any doubt about which way the tide was flowing.

Now, in the nineties, the movement is all the other way. In housing and in social services, it is the state which is on the retreat and in the process changing its role – in the current cliché, from providing to enabling. As a direct result, the voluntary sector has had to adapt – even reinvent – itself, in order to carry out the tasks with which it is being entrusted.

This process of adaptation is proving controversial – even painful, at times. The pessimists say that in taking on (or resuming) responsibilities for mainstream service provision, the voluntary sector risks forfeiting those characteristics that make it distinctive. As a junior partner in the welfare coalition, voluntary agencies could afford to be innovative and experimental. Risk taking was positively virtuous, with a safety net of statutory provision securely in place. But once they become the main source of provision, with responsibility for providing comprehensive coverage, voluntary organisations find themselves in the same position that the statutory agencies once occupied and have to accustom themselves to the same kinds of pressures and criticisms if they fail to deliver to the standard that users expect of public services. In these circumstances, the outcome is too often (pessimists say) that the voluntary bodies assume the form and style of the agencies they have replaced. The sociologists have an ugly word for this: isomorphism.

The optimists have a different story. They say that these changes are part of a broader process of transformation in our society (and other developed Western societies). Large bureaucracies providing uniform services of mediocre quality to an obediently passive population are a thing of the past – and good riddance.

Customers for welfare bring the same standards to their consumption of public services as they do to their supermarket shopping expeditions. They expect good quality provision and a choice of alternative forms of provision, with sufficient information to enable them to make intelligent decisions about which to take. They expect services of professional standard from a responsive and courteous staff. Voluntary agencies, the optimists suggest, are particularly well placed to provide services of this kind, with their traditions of flexibility, responsiveness and close relationship with the recipients of their services.

It is possible to overstate the case. Social services are not like supermarket products – they do not involve a single purchase, but often mean entering a continuing relationship with lasting implications for both parties. Choice is not always empowering – it can confuse and confusion can be exploited (as we have seen with the sale of personal pensions). Voluntary organisations are not always responsive to their users' needs and open to their demands. Many people know from personal experience that charitable status is not an automatic badge of virtue.

The important thing is that an opportunity now exists to redefine the role of voluntary action in the new circumstances of the last decade of the century. For a good long while now, the voluntary sector had made the assumption that the public will accept them at their own valuation. The belief had been reinforced by the apparent willingness of ordinary people to continue to give to charitable causes. Although the level of individual and corporate giving is in fact not particularly high in this country, the image persists of a collective willingness to support voluntary action – if only through the medium of lottery scratch cards.

Charitable gestures, by themselves, are not going to be enough to fill the space left by the retreat of the state. Those who like to believe, as some American politicians appear to do, that the welfare state can simply be abolished and that voluntary effort will expand naturally and evenly to fill the vacuum left, are the victims of a profound delusion about the nature of the voluntary effort and its limits as well as its capacities. The Webbs (who were often wrong) were right in pointing that out in their campaign for poor law reform at the beginning of this century.

Nevertheless, there is an important opportunity waiting to be grasped. At a time when the role of voluntary bodies is changing so fundamentally, it is vital that we stop being soft-hearted about voluntarism and start being hard-hearted about the new tasks that will have to be addressed and how they should be tackled. That is the job that the National Council for Voluntary Organisations (NCVO) has established its Commission on the future of voluntary action to undertake.

NICHOLAS DEAKIN
Professor of Social Policy and Social Administration at the University of Birmingham. Chair of the Commission of Inquiry into the Future of the Voluntary Sector

INTRODUCTION

John Crawley

On behalf of The Friendship Group, I should like to commend to the reader this, the publication of the first of our annual lectures on social change. These lectures are jointly sponsored by Friendship and our associated charity, Friendship Community Trust, in memory of Sarah Gibbs. Each year, we will choose a topical social issue of critical concern to the changing nature of British society as we approach the millennium.

The issue of community care was chosen because it is both the subject of considerable debate and controversy at present and because it is a central feature of Friendship's own work. That interest and commitment goes back to our origins in the 1950s when we provided what we today term supported housing.

In the 1980s, we extended our work in this field considerably with the start of those services – for people with learning difficulties, for mental health service users and for frail older people – which are our largest areas of activity today. Our services for elders include a registered care home in south Birmingham catering particularly for the needs and preferences of African-Caribbean elders, the kind of culturally sensitive service we are rather belatedly seeing emerge in Britain in response to the changing age profile and expectations of the minority ethnic communities. Designed to maximise the privacy and autonomy of service users, each of whom has their own fully self-contained flat, this service reflects Friendship's overall approach to service development. We take time to identify the precise nature of the need, and we ensure that our services are carefully tailored to the needs and preferences of prospective users and will maximise independence in the local community, rather than foster dependency in a closed institution. This elders' service is linked to an elders' day centre in the north of the city; here the people using our services have the crucial say over *how* it is run, another strong theme in our delivery of personal care services.

Two years ago, we established our group structure – Friendship Care Choices (FCC) is our community care agency with a distinct identity and operating independently of our main housing arm, Friendship Housing, and the traditional housing management services it provides. This step was in response to developments initiated by the recent community care legislation. FCC provides those of its service users who are also Friendship tenants with high quality professional care and support services whilst safeguarding their independent rights as tenants of Friendship.

At the same time, FCC has been developing an imaginative range of home support services for people who are not tenants of Friendship but need personal services to continue living in their own home. The emphasis is upon a flexible service for people living alone or with carers, with support shaped to suit their individual and unique circumstances. The service is responsive to change, is of high quality and is available 24 hours a day every day of the year.

Let me give you two examples of how it is used: a young woman with learning difficulties needs regular support to live on her own. The home support service provides a worker who gives support three times a week to assist with daily tasks such as money and household management, and acts as an advocate to support the young woman, ensuring she gains her rightful access to the other services she needs to sustain her independence.

The second example is of an elderly carer supporting her 40-year-old son who has multiple disabilities. With the family using our service the carer can have a regular weekly break at a time that *she* decides. When she is unwell the family can use the service daily to assist in the personal care and support management her son requires.

In short, the service gives real choice to people who require support to live their lives the way *they* want to, the essential aim behind all community care.

Friendship's philosophy can be summarised as responding positively to the diversity of social and individual needs we identify, placing strong emphasis upon the active involvement of people who use our services at all levels of the organisation. I was particularly pleased that our guests who joined us for Polly Toynbee's lecture included tenants and service users.

We are working in partnership with our colleagues in the statutory agencies, voluntary organisations and housing associations; with the latter, Friendship teams up with other housing associations where they can provide the homes and FCC can provide the support services, thus expanding access to such essential services. All of these partners were represented at the lecture. You can see the high quality of their contributions in the free-flowing debate with Polly which followed her lecture and which we have reproduced in Part Two of this book.

We aim to be a pacesetter organisation in community care and other fields. We are equally keen to be an open learning organisation, alert to new thinking and new ideas. This lecture series is a reflection of that spirit of enquiry.

JOHN CRAWLEY
Chief Executive of The Friendship Group

PART ONE

DO YOU WANT the good news or the bad news? The bad news first: there is a mounting crisis in caring for old people. The balance between those who work, pay taxes and contribute to pension funds, and those who do not work, who draw pensions and who need care is tipping. And the good news, you ask? The picture is a great deal darker in Japan and Germany, Sweden and France than it is here. There are many economists now – ever on the lookout for a silver lining – who say that this could be to Britain's long-term advantage, not only because these competitor nations will have to devote more of their resources to care, slowing up their economies, but also because those countries will need to import more goods as they will not have the workforce to produce them themselves, even with their advanced robotic skills.

But the media, as you know, likes bad news, so let me give you more of it. My generation constitutes a large proportion of the population. I won't give my exact date of birth quite yet, but let me say I am younger than Helen Mirren. I know she is older than me because once upon a time we were both in the National Youth Theatre together, and there was Helen, definitely older and a great star even then. But we were both, a year or two either way, a part of the post-war baby bulge, as it is inelegantly known. We are ageing – as the rapid growth of sales of anti-wrinkle creams demonstrates. We are a powerful generation with formidable earning and buying power on account of our size, but we bulge babies, as we reach 65, 70, 80, will start to need care. And who is going to pay for us when the time comes?

I was, I will confess it now, born in the

year that the NHS was set up, with Bevan's ringing promise, so fine, perhaps unrealisable, to care for all of us, forever, from the cradle to the grave. Already that promise is being broken in health authorities all over the country, not necessarily because of bad management, not necessarily because of Tory cuts either, but because it is a promise inherently unaffordable.

The ageing population

At the start of the National Health Service only one per cent of people lived to get really old, that is into their eighties. Very few lived to receive telegrams from the Queen on their hundredth birthday, but now she's sending them out by the bag-full. Maybe in some royal household cost-cutting scheme she will soon be sending them by fax or by E-mail.

For the numbers of the really old are surging. In 1981 2.8 per cent of the British population were aged over 80. By the year 2011 that proportion will have doubled.

Roman Catholics have a prayer for, indeed a patron saint, to oversee a happy death. We all hope for, in my experience both for ourselves and for our loved ones, a longer and longer life but, when it ends, for death to be short. The demographic fact is that people do seem to stay fit much longer than they used to do, but alas that the numbers of those needing nursing care for considerable periods of time are also growing.

Those are the quantities. But there is also a qualitative dimension to this. The nursing care that we – society – expects these days is of an ever-increasing standard. Dumping the old like rows of vegetables in Nightingale wards, crammed together too closely, with beds cheek-by-jowl, is no longer acceptable. Myself and colleagues in the media have helped to make it so on your behalf; we simply expect better. As our standards and expectations rise, for life, consumption, leisure, so we demand in turn that the elderly be treated with more dignity, and at great cost.

Geriatrics, still something of a Cinderella specialism in medicine, scarcely existed 25 years ago. Why? Because no-one thought it worth ensuring that old people in hospital were cured of incontinence or kept intellectually stimulated. Now we expect geriatricians to do everything they can, which these days is a great deal, to keep people as well, happy and alert as possible.

All of which means the NHS is faced with a far greater bill for the old than was ever expected when Nye Bevan promised care from cradle to grave for all. Bluntly put, the elderly are already consuming 60 per cent of the resources provided for the National Health Service. You could say that in terms of the life cycle there is nothing unreasonable about that proportion. For most of our lives most of us willingly pay taxes, which feed into NHS revenue, yet our use of health services is limited. We think in Beveridge's terms, as if the system were insurance based, which, of course, it is not, so that when we grow old we think we should be able to call in the chips and expect the system to be there for us. But is it?

'Community' care

Long-stay geriatric beds have been closing in their thousands. Behind that lies policy: by closing so many wards, health authorities, as ever short of cash, have seen a way of shifting the burden off their budgets because now there is an alternative provider – and this isn't going to be its only appearance here – that class act, imprecise, protean, star of both Left and Right at the moment: the community.

You will forgive my heavy irony but I have become deeply suspicious of that word. Yet it is everywhere, on the lips of all the political parties. John Major and Tony Blair, not to mention Paddy Ashdown, have fallen over themselves to lay claim to the concept of community. American gurus are given red carpet treatment preaching a pious – and some think – rather threatening doctrine of community activism. The word rings through the political discourse of the 1990s. But not with me, because whenever I hear it I stop and ask: 'Who, where, how? Who is community? Where is community? How is community?' And I will tell you what you already know. Community is predominantly female carers, at home, unpaid and unsung. Where is community? It is hard to define where there are places in modern Britain with which people still strongly identify.

Sir John Banham does not know, and he, as Chairman of the Local Government Commission spent two years and £12 million of public money going round the country asking people, 'Which community do you belong to?' The answers are often very incoherent. It turns out place, or community, is a very weak identifier in the modern world. Job and family, friends and interests, matter far more. So when it comes to a policy demanding that 'the community' cares for people no longer cared for by the NHS, I worry.

Changes in funding

Until the late 1980s there were three different budgets that might be called upon to pay for nursing care of the old. If NHS beds were in short supply, local authority social services departments would step in and provide places in council-run homes. Alternatively beds might be funded centrally through the Department of Social Security's budget and provided in, for example, private-sector run establishments.

Then came Sir Roy Griffiths, who was commissioned to report, and on the basis of his recommendations the Community Care Act was passed. Funding for care of the old from the centre through social security was stopped. A re-apportionment of funds was set in train, money being channelled to local authority social services. In principle that was a right and sensible rationalisation.

However, the government never really got to grips with the way responsibility divided between the National Health Service and the local authorities. Many sincere people put a lot of time and effort into attempting to make that division of labour work, and in some areas the two sides do work very closely and well together. But the fact is that all the financial imperatives say: compete. The system is designed to try to encourage each to push responsibility for care onto the other. For reasons of ideology – ie, Mrs Thatcher's problems with local authorities – the Community Care Act did not entrust them with full responsibility, nor did it dare to give the whole budget to the NHS, for fear of taking even more power away from local government. Perhaps no clear dividing line could ever be drawn: there would always be a large grey area surrounding the condition of a person who may be a patient in need of medical attention, but who may be merely frail and in need of care and not doctoring. The story could have ended here. It would be a matter of internal organisation, not particularly fascinating except to those who work in the services.

Responses to change

Community care has suddenly become high politics. What happens to the old has recently become a matter of the keenest interest to a very great number of people who have only suddenly woken up to some stark financial facts, and because they are upset, of even keener interest to the party strategists. By law, the NHS is not allowed to charge fees for care, but once a person falls into the clutches of social services, then he or she will be expected to pay according to their means, which could mean almost down to their last penny. In principle this has always been so: social services have always been allowed to seek to claw back contributions towards the cost of care from those who could afford it. It has been the demise of the long-stay hospital bed that has brought this financial fact into a new sharper focus. Most families have now no option but to pay as they can no longer choose a free hospital bed instead. Also until recently many fewer old people had capital assets and homes to sell in order to pay for their care.

A growing awareness of relatives that they will have to pay, or see the assets of their mother or father liquidated has created a political problem of huge significance. Stories are rumbling through the press. It is another potential tumbril for a government in mortal fear of losing more middle-class support in the run-up to the next General Election. *The Express* and *The Sunday Times* have run vociferous campaigns on this subject.

The argument is based on disappointed expectations. The argument is that it is the state's duty to fulfil an old promise, that it would nurse the old until death – in other words, the NHS should pay, and all nursing care should be free to all who need it. This argument can be supported with some pretty horrific examples: people I have come across myself. There are plenty of cases of people who have had severe strokes or other deeply disabling conditions who have been turfed out of hospital beds on the grounds that there is no cure that medicine can offer. These are people who, whatever the technicalities of financing, are quadriplegic, bed-ridden, unable to speak or feed themselves. They need 24-hour nursing and certainly look like hospital patients, and not like nursing home residents. Two decades ago no-one would have considered rejecting them from the NHS. Now, following a new Department of Health directive they have lost their fight to refuse to go.

Once in nursing homes, anyone with savings or assets over £8,000 has to pay all the rest towards their upkeep. They have to sell the homes to which they will now never return. An average priced house, worth perhaps £50,000, can be swallowed up easily within five years in paying the nursing home bills and will leave the pensioner with virtually nothing.

'Pillaging the fruits of a lifetime's toil', one newspaper has called it. Prudent old people who spent their life saving and paying off the mortgage believed they were building up a nest-egg to hand on to their children and grandchildren, to help them buy houses too. Rashly, John Major promised a cascade of wealth down the generations. Indeed the government is also thinking of raising the inheritance tax threshold from £150,000 to £250,000 in order to bolster this ideal of inheritance. That will not cut much ice with the growing battalions of outraged families who see their inheritance cascade pouring into the coffers of the Treasury instead.

Why, they clamour, should anyone now bother to save? Before you get old, give away your money quickly, spend, spend, spend, throw prudence to the wind and enjoy it while you can, because otherwise it will only go to pay for care you would get free if you did not have the money. It penalises the wise and rewards the feckless.

What is more, they complain with some justification, how unfair life is that the burden falls unevenly and uncertainly. After all, only a small proportion of the old will need expensive residential care for any length of time. The rest, who die after a short illness, get to pass their nest-eggs onto the children intact. Surely, they say, the NHS was devised in order to even out the injustices of fate, and to ensure that illness does not lead to penury, with the risks and costs spread evenly across the whole population.

Agendas for care

By the turn of the century, 700,000 people will be in residential or nursing homes. Most of them will be home owners who were encouraged to buy into the property-owning democracy by a government that believes in the value of allowing wealth to be inherited. They will see their homes vanish. They and their children and grandchildren form a threateningly large number of voters, to say nothing of the hundreds of thousands of others who live in fear of it happening to them. The word is that Downing Street is looking at these figures and taking fright – alarmed at the clamour in the right wing press, they want to find a quick-fix way out.

There are various suggestions, the most expensive of which would be to allow old people to put the capital value of their house into a trust. The interest would contribute towards their care bills, the capital would stay secure to pass on to their children. This would mean, of course, that they would be contributing a tiny fraction of what they pay now towards their care. It is estimated that it would cost some £500 million right now, but imagine how that cost will soar by the time my generation gets into its dotage.

Other proposals include the idea that people could buy their place in a nursing home with their capital, and then after their death their children could sell it on to some other old person and realise their inheritance. That, too, would mean a great deal more money being spent on care by the government.

Then there is a proposal for various tax-free savings bonds in which people can budget ahead for their care costs, but anything that is tax-free also costs the Exchequer considerable sums in tax foregone. It is suggested that the time has come for some compulsory pension scheme to ensure people are better provided for in their old age – whether run by the state or by private firms, people should be made to save more. Too many people imagine still that the state will provide, but by the time I retire the state pension is likely to have withered away to virtually nothing, whoever is in power. Compulsion may be the only way, for if people feel their savings will be eaten up in care costs, they may be reluctant to fork out voluntarily for something many still feel strongly should be paid for by the state.

There is something very curious about this campaign in the right-wing press. It would be far more understandable if it came from the Left. It is the Right that has tried to cut back on state power and state handouts, the Right that encourages private and individual provision. Now suddenly they want the state to spend millions, which would soon turn into billions more, of taxpayers' money.

But we must remember that the amount of money that can be raised in taxes by any government in a democracy is more or less constant. People will rebel and refuse to elect governments they suspect will tax them beyond what they think they can bear to pay, though they may be nudged or tricked into paying a little more from time to time. 'Watch My Lips, No More Taxes' has become the universal cry of any party in the western world that stands a chance of getting elected. Promises may be broken later, as by this government, or by George Bush who will be remembered by those words if for little else, but broadly the sums raised by the Exchequer are not likely to swell significantly whoever is in power.

In which case we must always talk the language of priorities. Now, how high a priority should we give to free care of the elderly? Asked bluntly, most people would probably say it should have a very high priority. But let's ask it another way. How high a priority should we give people's ability to hand down to their children their homes and capital. After all, those who stand to gain are mostly couples in their fifties who have already brought up their children, who have bought their own home – do they really need a large windfall at that stage in their lives? What for? For cruises, for a rather luxurious early retirement? They already have more disposable income for the least expensive stage in their lives than ever before. In terms of organising the economy, it seems curious to spend government money on these people who need it least as a high priority.

Competing priorities

Look around us, and everywhere we see the desperate need for more expenditure. Many of the poorest of the elderly need far more help in their own homes. The young, who will pay for our pensions and care in the future, need to be educated so they can compete successfully against the economies of better educated nations. The health service needs money to pay for ever more expensive drugs and new technologies. The unemployed need training. The inner cities need rejuvenating. The list is painfully long.

So where, in the scheme of things, would you place the rights of the better off, middle-aged to inherit houses? Why should these causes lose out to ensure old people keep money that is no longer of use to them, while the taxpayer foots the bill for their care? There are many in government who do not think it would be right or fair. Social Security ministers are said to be against it. But if the political dictates of a government in severe electoral distress lead us down that path, it will be an act of extra-ordinary cynicism. It will be giving in to a lobby of the rich against the interests of the poor.

However, there is one aspect of all this

that is far from clear cut. If we step back from it for a minute and examine exactly what has happened, it ought to ring some alarm bells for the future. The political storm about paying for the care of the elderly, either in their own home or in residential and nursing homes, has blown up suddenly because it has taken people unawares. Slyly, by the back door, with no political debate or public discussion, a major change was made in the contract between the NHS and the people, without their consent. Politicians, over the years, by stealth, have closed the long-stay NHS wards and before people understood its significance, the guarantee of free nursing care for all had been withdrawn.

Now this may act as a model for further withdrawals of treatment by the NHS. The funds are limited, the demands on it are growing at twice the rate of inflation, partly because of the ageing population, partly because of the galloping costs of new treatments. Popular pressure is for everything, however expensive, to be offered to everyone, even if the chances of success of some new treatments are very slight. If some child does not get a state of the art treatment costing tens of thousands of pounds from which they may only have a tiny chance of recovery, the press rises up in outcry. In order to shame the NHS it urges the public to subscribe to send the child, like Laura Davies, to America for seven organ transplants.

Making choices

The public demands that the NHS provides everything. Yet it looks, increasingly, as if it cannot. It has shed a large burden in escaping from caring for the old, but what will it shed next? The system of rationing used to be by waiting lists, but the Patients' Charter targets have forced the pace. Now health authorities are casting around for other ways to limit treatments on offer. But where is the public debate? Where is the consultation and the political process?

The public is encouraged to behave in a childish way in its attitude towards the NHS because no-one dares put the problem fairly and squarely in an adult way. Politicians of all parties are so afraid of the sacred trust people have in the health service that they will not discuss it honestly. Yet discussion of rationing is essential, both in terms of treatment and in terms, I suspect, of care. Or, if the word rationing is too stark, then at least the setting of priorities. People need to think hard about the huge cost of keeping a baby alive under 23-weeks' gestation with a high chance of handicap, and then weigh that against, perhaps, half-a-dozen hip replacements that will lift six old people out of wheelchairs and give them a good many pain-free and active years.

Health economists have devised a scheme of points, called QUALYS, or Quality Adjusted Life Years, which they apportion to medical treatments. They assess how many good years of comfort can be bought per pound spent on any treatment, and that produces an interesting scale.

But perhaps we are not yet ready for such rationality. Perhaps we prefer the old system of hidden rationing when the consultant would say: 'This is the right treatment for you.' And you would trust his word. No-one ever knew whether money came into his decision; no-one ever knew whether better could be had elsewhere. We shut our eyes and believed in doctors, and, who knows, perhaps we preferred it that way in more innocent days.

But one of the most profound effects of the health service reforms has been to make patients keenly aware of money, suspicious that it does affect their treatment, and more wary of doctors. The level of complaint has risen many-fold for this reason. For this reason, too, I do not think the public can be kept out of the decision-making processes of priority setting within the NHS and within social services for very much longer. The debate happens, piecemeal, over every notorious case, but someone, somewhere, has to be brave enough to take these issues into the public domain in order to obtain some kind of workable consensus.

I have wandered some distance from community care, but all these issues are bound up together. There really is no difference, it seems to me, between medical and nursing care. It is an arbitrary, bureaucratic demarcation. Old people have needs of all kinds. The attentions of a good geriatrition can make a vast difference to their quality of life, so can meals-on-wheels; and so can a home care service or a nursing home that treats them with kindness and respect. All these things we need more of, and the need will grow. We have to ensure that for the future we have created a secure financial base with which to pay for them.

Above all, we have to make sure that we target the finite sources that we have on those who need it most, and that money is not wasted by cynical politicians seeking short-term electoral gain at horrendous cost to the care of present and future generations.

PART TWO

Polly Toynbee:
Questions and answers.

You have talked about the need for a public debate about the future of care for older people. Who should debate this question, and where would the debate be conducted?

The debate has to be grasped by the government in power. This government feels that it cannot, because it is not trusted on the NHS, and it is not trusted on social services. A new Labour government could seize the opportunity to talk for the first time honestly about priorities. They could say, 'We think there is something very unfair about how different the provision is up and down the country and we should have some national debate about what people really want provided.' Why should you be able to get IVF treatment in one place and not another, for instance? And it is certainly true with social services that you can get some things in some places and not in others. There is something very arbitrary about that.

There should be an honest national debate led by a government that was actually listening to what was being said all over the country. You might then end up with a system which people would consent to, and even participate in. Obviously in a democracy not everybody can have their say, but we could try a lot harder than politicians have. Up to now, they have just pretended there is no need to discuss it because any admission of failure is just bounced back on them by the opposition. A new government does not take on the responsibilities for existing failures, and to some extent can start with a clean slate. Such a debate does need to be coupled with returning power to local authorities even though it is difficult to balance local decision-making with fairness across the country.

Is there any way that we can enlist the media into a constructive exercise of debating the priorities for public expenditure on different medical and social conditions?

I don't think so. We have got to live with the media we've got, whether we deserve it or not. I don't see that it is likely to change its structure or owner- ship or political direction very much.

In Oregon they did a survey on people's care priorities, and they didn't get the obvious answers. The elderly came out of it very well and new-born babies came out of it very badly. You might think everybody would say, 'Aah, lovely little babies.' But it didn't work that way. People made quite interesting, quite subtle choices. It was only used for guidelines; it wasn't a referendum on who lived or died. It was used as a tool for policy makers and politicians who had to make these difficult spending decisions.

In the end they have got to take the rap. Somebody has to and we pay them and elect them to do it. They have to make priority decisions for all the spending departments. We can't let them duck out by simply saying, 'We'll have a vote and you will decide and then it'll be your fault.' Ultimately these things have to be done by politicians. But politicians could do it better if they were to have an open discussion; to listen to what people have to say; and to explain better to people the nature of the decisions that they're having to make, rather than taking them secretively, behind closed doors and in a rather ramshackle way.

Rather than talking about making choices between competing priorities, would it not be better to spend time persuading the public to pay more in taxes?

It is always the way out of any problem to say, 'Let's raise taxes and persuade people.' But the Labour Party has done that at four elections, and it has not done very well. In fact at the last one, they weren't really saying they were going to raise taxes, but people thought they would. Being hard headed about it, it seems political suicide at the moment for any party in a western democracy to say, 'You should look after the weaker members of society. You should be willing to pay a little more.'

Most of us in work are doing better than ever before. We can afford to pay. So there is a very convincing case. But it just doesn't cut any ice. However eloquently it was put, it would be a suicidal campaign – honourable, noble, even uplifting in many ways, but the road to ruin. Everyone has got to realise that the pot is always going to be limited. If you did raise more, it would only be that little bit more – not enough to make a significant difference.

You said that the health service has never been adequately funded through the national insurance contribution system. If the ideal of that system was rediscovered so that the contributory system was clearly geared to the needs of these essential services, might this be a way of making deductions from pay more acceptable?

It might, particularly, as people are worried about costs of care, but when people stop and think about it, only a relatively small number of people will require care. So it is quickly going to be seen as another form of taxation.

I am not a great believer in the national insurance system because I think that anybody of about 40 or younger doesn't identify with it. Older people who remember it being set up understand the magnificent principle behind it and identify with it. Younger people haven't a clue what it means – it is simply another bit off your wages. It has no resonance. They do not understand the difference between means-tested benefits, ones you are entitled to through national insurance, and ones you get anyway, like Child Benefit.

But they do understand about the pension – 'I know I'm paying into my pension' – and if there is no pension fund they're rather shocked. When it is pointed out to them that they have absolutely no rights on any future pension, that what they're paying for is current pensions, and there may be very little for them when they become pensioners themselves, a huge hole has been blown right through the national insurance principle. You would need to start all over again with a completely different idea of it.

Most politicians when they look at the workings of the national insurance system would like to demolish it. They are afraid to do so because it would add something like another seven to eight pence on income tax. So the opposition party would immediately put out the headline: 'Government adds 8p to income tax.' The fact that it was being taken away from national insurance wouldn't be properly understood. So for reasons of political cowardice, it has never been rationalised. But it should be as part of a major overhaul of the way we look at benefits.

I know this is rather iconoclastic, but I don't think my mother, who is quite well off, should be having a state pension, and I don't think I should be drawing Child Benefit. If I was Social Security minister I would resent paying out ever larger sums to pensioners who now have quite good private pensions themselves. I would want to take that money and target it on the poorest set of pensioners who have nothing. I would take the money from quite well-off families and give it to the children who have nothing. The day of the universal benefit is over, because it's costing too much paying it out to too many people who do not need it.

Should children be compelled to take responsibility for the care of their elderly parents?

That's a very interesting question. In Germany they do make children pay for parents. In Britain you may take away prospective inheritance, but you can't actually touch children for money for their parents' care. In Germany they can. Families are thought to be responsible. Even if your father beat you black and blue and nearly killed you as a child, they can come out and find you when he's 85 and say you've got to pay, regardless of what the relationship is. That's quite wrong — it's going too far.

I don't wish to see the family institutionalised in that way, without any sensitivity to the incredibly complex relationships that go on in the name of family. The most frightful things happen inside families and the idea that we all love each other and should pay for each other regardless, seems to me wrong, fundamentally wrong.

Do you see some particular role for voluntary organisations in the provision of public services?

It's very difficult because they often do it so well. On the other hand the voluntary sector is increasingly becoming a vast business with very little freedom to provide services in an individualistic way. As time goes on it will become more institutionalised and more like local authority services used to be. The voluntary principle will disappear.

One of the great strengths in our society is the voluntary sector – people being willing to do things out of the best possible motives and instincts. If it becomes entirely professionalised, people won't stop being interested in charity, but it blurs the line quite dangerously. I don't know what the answer is because they are obviously providing good services. It is good to have a diversity of providers to keep standards up, to keep things in competition, to have people constantly trying to get the best possible services for the money, but I think there are great dangers for a lot of splendid organisations.

Even if some of the staff of voluntary organisations are paid, isn't it a very important aspect of community participation that there should be plenty of opportunities for people to offer their services voluntarily to their local community?

I would absolutely agree with that, but

the danger is that some of the bigger ones just become more and more managerial. As long as you can keep the local link so people keep the sense that this is 'our' organisation, 'we're' providing the services for our local people in the way we want, that's magnificent. But if you get vast nationwide organisations, they lose touch with their roots quite quickly.

Any sense of community involvement in urban settings is so difficult these days. The Henley Centre for Forecasting not long ago produced some figures which were pretty horrifying. The number of people who ever volunteered for anything is tiny and shrinking. It's not that people are particularly selfish. Nobody asks them – there isn't an avenue by which they can be drawn in. They don't have a good friend who is doing it who says one day 'Come along'. I think an awful lot of people would like to do it if it was presented to them in a way that fitted in with their lives, and with their own sort of people.

There's a resource to be tapped into, but it is very difficult. With this lovely word 'community' people easily gloss over quite how difficult it is to make urban society feel at all like a community. Even if you set up a little community radio station, it helps a bit. But then you look at the people who are actually being involved, and who actually tunes in. It's still pretty small.

You need a range of activities and hope that somehow you get people to participate somewhere in something. Even so, when you do it's still quite likely to be a very small part of their perception of themselves and the world they live in. They might do some activity one night a week, but that doesn't necessarily identify that person as being 'of the community'. That is one thing they do, but there are also a lot of others – a job, a family – and if they come from somewhere else that family may be far away.

It is terribly easy to be nostalgic and sentimental and unrealistic. The danger is that it sets up a lot of projects for terrible disappointment and bitterness. People then ask, 'Why won't they all come together?' One of the reasons people like living in cities is because they want to choose their own communities amongst friends that they can choose and not be forced to have to live together with a whole street of neighbours they may detest. There is a lot to be said for the non-community of city life. And a lot can be said against the old days with everybody looking through net curtains at everybody else. It had a certain discipline – if you got pregnant and you weren't married, all hell broke loose and your life was made a nightmare. It kept a certain social order, but at an incredibly high cost to human happiness.

Do you think that the voluntary sector could play a bigger role in the provision of care for older people, for example, as was done with the hospice movement?

There are corners – things the NHS has never done – where there is room for the voluntary sector to move in and develop something of its own. But it has to be something new. It would not be acceptable for the NHS to say, 'We're not going to do this any more. You do it.' People would not contribute funds to that.

The point about the hospice movement was that it was a totally new concept with a very charismatic leader, with a very clear message. Everybody is desperately worried about death and knows that hospital death was very unsatisfactory, and often had bad experiences of relatives dying in completely the wrong ways and in the wrong settings. It was a niche that somebody could step into afresh.

I do not see bits of the NHS or social services being hived off in quite that way – the voluntary sector as providers, yes, but not taking on the total financial responsibility for something that is already provided by the state.

There is an argument that if you develop resources for those in acute and greatest need – the minority – you deny resources to the majority for preventative care and assistance. Could you comment on that?

I am always very depressed about how remote that possibility is. In all the years that I have been writing about social issues, so many papers have come out saying if we could only divert money towards prevention, then we could save ourselves a great deal of money in the long run and keep people more independent for longer. But I have yet to see any sign of anyone taking money away from the acute end of things and putting it into prevention. It just does seem to be extremely difficult politically. I am not aware of a local authority, let alone a government that has bitten on the bullet and said: 'All right, some people at the sharp end are really going to suffer, but at least a lot of other people will be better off.'

Do you think that if our legislation on equal opportunities was extended to older people this would allow them a bigger bite of the cherry?

It might do something for younger old people, in terms of employment and discrimination of that kind. Equal opportunities legislation has never been used to shift resources in a big way in this country, and I cannot see how it ever could be.

Equal opportunities legislation is used as a kind of beacon, an indicator, as a warning, and as a tool that people can use to try and change public attitudes. But large sums of money do not necessarily shift as a result.

Do you think that because there is no special legislation on the subject, the authorities choose not to spend money?

There is a limit to the amount of legislation you want. Local authorities already have so little freedom of action, that if you ring fence absolutely every-thing, there is virtually nothing left to local government. Do we want to tie their hands even further ?

I would rather go the other way and give them more discretion, more accoun-tability to make people feel more involved in their local government. The more we can get down to the local level, the better decisions might be, and the more people might engage with the real issues of priorities. Issues need to be tangible and clear to people on their own doorstep when they can see people close to them − their own councillors −

actually making decisions rather than obeying government instructions.

Do you think things were better before the community care legislation and NHS reforms?

I am concerned that there is a danger of looking back to the days of asylums and similar institutions as if they were part of a Golden Age.

I did not want you to think I would like to go back to that necessarily. I have said most people want to be in their own homes, and there were an awful lot of people put into institutions who could have managed in their own homes. No. It is this question of choice.

I certainly also didn't want to give the impression that I had a rosy view of what the NHS was like before. I am not of the school that says they were great old days and it was all wonderful. I think people were much happier with it before, because they didn't understand how it worked so well. From the government's point of view, the great disaster of its health reforms politically is to take away peoples' confidence, even if it has succeeded in improving a number of things.

A lot of the old NHS was a con trick. It was not justifiable confidence. A lot of it was terrible, so I do not regard the health service as having been destroyed by the reforms. What has happened has been very interesting. Some things may be worse, but I think quite a lot are better.

Do you think that the original aims of care in the community are being realised in relation to the mentally ill, in particular those people who have schizophrenia?

There's a deep divide amongst families of those with schizophrenia, between the people on the Marjory Wallace side of the argument who support the organisation SANE and those who come more from the MIND view of it. I find myself very persuaded by what Marjory Wallace says about how there is a great need for more beds in mental hospitals for people to be kept in longer. This is a return to the idea of asylum, which originally was a generous idea of a place where people are protected, not necessarily locked away for life, but a place that will always be there for you in the acute phase of illness. Families are relieved of the appalling burden of relatives when they are in a terrible state. They will be treated kindly and will come back to the community when it is at all possible.

The rush for community care was at its sharpest and cruellest in the closure of mental hospitals. A lot of them were dreadful places. I've visited some that were just appalling. Even so, they weren't that dreadful, and they were certainly less dreadful than the street, than suicide and all of the other things that can happen.

People are very unwilling to spend money on the mentally ill, particularly schizophrenics who frighten them. That's why you have to be careful with the idea of a democratic checklist – because of the people who would fall to the bottom of it every time. You do need a firm government that says, 'We don't just give to the most charming patients.'

On the other hand community care has been wonderful for a lot of people

who are now managing amazingly independent lives that nobody would have
thought of 30 years ago. But there are
cases of people suffering very severely
who have been dumped in the community.

*If we look at community care, doesn't its
success depend not on volunteers but on
how much money is spent?*

Care has become associated with money.
It is what you expect the state, or the
state via other agencies, to provide.
'Care' is one of those words that can
disappear into something that's pretty
seedy. A lot of what passes for care is
minimal and quite appalling.

The whole idea of 'the care package
which is right for you' draws a wry laugh
from a lot of places. It's been a peculiar
way of going about things to have your

needs assessed but then to be told that there's nothing or virtually nothing on offer. It is raising people's expectations, but then not giving them any minimum guarantee of the treatment they can expect according to whatever condition it is that they're in.

The emphasis on community care has kept a lot more people in their homes, but I am waiting for the spate – and I fear it will happen at some point – of a lot of rather nasty cases of people dying in their own homes in pretty unpleasant conditions with nobody having noticed. With those authorities that are rather bad at it, the policy may begin to fall apart at the seams and we may have to move to some system that does give minimum guarantees as there was in the past. If your family or anybody else thought you weren't coping, you could go into residential care and central govern-

ttle more cautious and a little less
clined to think of renting as a bad thing.
n not a housing economist, but I don't
e where the major investment in
nting is going to come from, at least
t without some kind of subsidy — and
t in itself will present distortions.

ment would pay. Now that that guarantee
has been removed, there must be a lot of
people out there in considerable peril in
some areas.

*Why is it so difficult to get public discussion
about social housing, even in relation to the
homeless?*

Homelessness has been perceived as
being about people on the streets, and
kids being thrown out of homes and, to
some extent, about the mentally ill
fetching up on the streets. It never really
turned into a full-scale housing debate
looking at the structure of how we invest
in housing. There have been stabs at it —
like looking at mortgage tax relief.

There is something very odd about
the way social issues become very
fashionable and then disappear. But they

certainly do come and go. Often it is the initiative of a few people who suddenly seize the right moment and the right issue who can make that issue become tremendously dominant. What's interesting, when you look around Europe, is that very often people are thinking about quite different social problems, despite having more or less the same problems and the same economic structure. And this is puzzling. For example, they're desperately worried about drugs when we're only moderately worried about drugs. Quite often though, inspirational leadership makes a big difference, as Des Wilson did once for housing.

With the cris
negative equ
home-owner
trend towa
homes?

People wh
optimisti
such a be
I can't r
many p
proper
how w
rented
gover
rente
our
amo
buyi

I
ow
fro

I N D E X

Index

Index

Index